Tottenham

Quiz Book
101 Questions That Will Test Your Knowledge
Of This Historic Football Club

Published by Glowworm Press
7 Nuffield Way
Abingdon OX14 1RL

By Chris Carpenter

Tottenham Hotspur Quiz Book

This book contains one hundred and one informative and entertaining trivia questions with multiple choice answers. With 101 questions, some easy, some more challenging, this book will test your knowledge and memory of the club's long and successful history. The book is packed with information and is a must-have for all loyal Spurs supporters. You will be asked a wide range of wonderful questions on a wide range of topics associated with **Tottenham Hotspur Football Club** for you to test yourself.

You will be quizzed on players, legends, managers, opponents, transfer deals, trophies, records, honours, fixtures, songs and much more, guaranteeing you an educational experience. Educational, enjoyable and fun, this quiz book will provide the ultimate in entertainment for Spurs fans of all ages.

2019/20 Season Edition

FOREWORD

When I was asked to write a foreword to this book I was flattered.

I have known the author Chris Carpenter for a number of years and his knowledge of facts and figures is phenomenal.

His love for football and his skill in writing quiz books make him the ideal man to pay homage to my great love Tottenham Hotspur Football Club.

This book came about as a result of a challenge on a golf course.

I do hope you enjoy the book.

Terry Wilson

Let's start with some relatively easy questions.

1. In which year was Tottenham Hotspur founded?
    A. 1880
    B. 1882
    C. 1884

2. What is the club's nickname?
    A. Lilys
    B. Roosters
    C. Spurs

3. Who is Tottenham Hotspur's current manager?
    A. Mauricio Pochettino
    B. Tim Sherwood
    C. Andre Villas-Boas

4. Who holds the record for making the most number of appearances?
    A. Pat Jennings
    B. Gary Mabbutt
    C. Steve Perryman

5. Who holds the record for being the all-time top goal scorer?
    A. Martin Chivers
    B. Jimmy Greaves
    C. Bobby Smith

6. Who has the record for most goals in a season?

A. Clive Allen
B. Dimitar Berbatov
C. Jermain Defoe

7. What is the name of Tottenham Hotspur's mascot?
    A. Chirpy Cockerel
    B. Charlie Cock
    C. Roger Rooster

8. Which player has scored the fastest ever goal for the club?
    A. Robbie Keane
    B. Ledley King
    C. Gary Lineker

9. What can be regarded as the fans' most well-known song?
    A. Glory Glory Tottenham Hotspur
    B. Spurs are on their way to Wembley
    C. Tottenham is my team

10.   Which of these three is a well known pub near the ground?
    A. The Elmhurst
    B. The Elms
    C. The Elm Tree

Here are the answers to the first ten questions. If you get seven or more right, you are doing well, but don't get too cocky, as the questions do get harder.

A1. Tottenham Hotspur was founded on 5th September 1882 as Hotspur FC. In 1884 the club was renamed Tottenham Hotspur Football Club to avoid any confusion with an already established team called Hotspur FC. The club played in the Southern League until 1908 when they were elected into the Football League Second Division.

A2. Spurs is the most common nickname of Tottenham Hotspur, although Lilywhites is also used, but not Lilys.

A3. Mauricio Roberto Pochettino started the 2019/20 season as manager. He was appointed to the role in May 2014.

A4. Steve Perryman made a record 854 appearances in total for the club between 1969 and 1986. Legend.

A5. Jimmy Greaves is Tottenham's highest ever goal scorer, finding the back of the net a record 266 times, including 220 times in the League.

A6. Clive Allen scored an incredible 49 goals in the 1986/87 season.

A7. Chirpy Cockerel is the official mascot.

A8. Ledley King scored the fastest ever goal for Tottenham Hotspur, just ten seconds after kick off in a Premier League match at Bradford City on 9th December 2000.

A9. "Glory Glory Tottenham Hotspur" is the most famous chant the fans sing. Other clubs' fans copy this chant, but Spurs were the first to sing it.

A10. The Elmhurst is a famous pub near White Hart Lane. Be prepared to queue for a pint though.

OK, let's have some questions about the ground.

11. Where does Tottenham Hotspur play their home games?
    A. White Angel Lane
    B. White Hart Lane
    C. White Lily Lane

12. In 1899, what was on the site of the ground?
    A. A colliery
    B. A monastery
    C. A nursery

13. What was the capacity of the ground before the recent re-development?
    A. 34,052
    B. 36,284
    C. 38,104

14. What is the capacity of the new redeveloped stadium?
    A. 60,505
    B. 61,599
    C. 62,062

15. What is the nearest tube station to the ground?
    A. Finsbury Park
    B. Seven Sisters
    C. Tottenham Hale

16. Who was the architect of the old ground?
    A. James Gillespie

B. Archibald Leitch
C. Robert McAlpine

17. Who is the architect of the new stadium?
A. Populina
B. Populist
C. Populous

18.   What is the size of the pitch?
A. 113 x 73 yards
B. 114 x 75 yards
C. 115 x 74 yards

19. What is Tottenham Hotspur's record home (non-Wembley) attendance?
A. 71,048
B. 73,058
C. 75,038

20.   Where is the club's training ground?
A. Edgware
B. Enfield
C. Epping

Here are the answers to the last set of questions.

A11. White Hart Lane is what everyone knows as home, although the new stadium will also be known as Tottenham Hotspur Stadium. Let's face it the name "Tottenham Hotspur Stadium" is temporary, the intention being to sell the naming rights, so that it will be named after a sponsor.

A12. The White Hart Lane ground was originally a disused nursery owned by the brewery Charringtons.

A13. The capacity of White Hart Lane the season before it was developed had been reduced to just 36,284, hence the need for a new stadium.

A14. The new stadium has a capacity of 62,062. It was officially opened on 3rd April 2019 before it staged its first competitive senior game, a Premier League match against Crystal Palace which Tottenham won 2-0, with Son Heung-min scoring the first ever official goal at the new stadium.

A15. White Hart Lane and Northumberland Park mainline overground train stations are less than ten minutes walk from the ground, but the nearest tube station is a brisk twenty minutes walk away at Tottenham Hale, although it's often easier to hop on a bus to and from Seven Sisters tube station.

A16. The original stadium at the Lane was designed by Archibald "Archie" Leitch, who at the time was Britain's foremost football architect.

A17. The new stadium at the Lane was designed by Populous which is a global architectural company specialising in sports arenas. If you have not been yet, you are in for a treat when you do go. It has been a long time in the making, and it is every bit as good as people say it is.

A18. The official size of the new pitch is 115 yards long and 74 yards wide, or if you prefer 105 metres by 68 metres. By way of comparison, the pitch at Wembley is 115 yards long and 75 yards wide.

A19. Tottenham Hotspur's record home attendance is 75,038, which was in an FA Cup tie on 5th March 1938 against Sunderland.

A20. Tottenham's training ground is on a 77 acres site at Bulls Cross, Enfield which is close to Junction 25 of the M25.

Here is the next set of questions.

21. What is the club's best ever finish in the
    Premier League?
    A. 2nd
    B. 3rd
    C. 4th

22.   What is the fewest number of goals that
    Tottenham Hotspur has conceded in a single
    Premier League season?
    A. 26
    B. 31
    C. 35

23.   What is the club's record win in any
    competition?
    A. 11-2
    B. 12-3
    C. 13-2

24.   What is the club's record win in the
    League?
    A. 7-0
    B. 8-0
    C. 9-0

25.   Which team did Tottenham Hotspur
    beat in their record League win?
    A. Blackburn Rovers
    B. Bristol City
    C. Bristol Rovers

26.   What is the club's record defeat?
    A. 0-6
    B. 0-7
    C. 0-8

27.   What is the highest number of goals that Tottenham Hotspur has scored in a single Premier League season?
    A. 68
    B. 71
    C. 74

28.   In which season did the club score two or more goals in every Champions League group game?
    A. 2009/10
    B. 2010/11
    C. 2011/12

29.   Which player has made the most number of Premier League appearances for the club?
    A. Darren Anderton
    B. Jermain Defoe
    C. Ledley King

30.   Which player has scored the most number of hat tricks for Tottenham Hotspur in the Premier League?
    A. Dimitar Berbatov
    B. Jermain Defoe
    C. Harry Kane

Here are the answers to the last block of questions.

A21. At the end of the 2016/17 season, Tottenham Hotspur recorded their highest ever Premier League finish – 2nd.

A22. Spurs conceded just 26 goals during the 2016/17 Premier League season. Their previous best defensive record was 35 goals, the season before.

A23. Tottenham Hotspur's record win is 13-2. Spurs defeated Crewe Alexandra in an FA Cup tie on 3rd February 1960. It is also the highest scoring FA Cup tie of the 20th century.

A24. Tottenham's record win in the League is 9-0, in the dark days while the club were playing in Division Two.

A25. Tottenham Hotspur defeated Bristol Rovers 9-0 on 22nd October 1977, in the 1977/78 season in their record league win. Colin Lee scored four goals. On his debut!

A26. Tottenham Hotspur suffered their worst ever defeat on 22nd July 1995, in an Intertoto match at the beginning of the 1995/96 season losing 0-8 against FC Koln of Germany. The Tottenham side was made up of reserves and youth team players. The goalkeeper was Chris Day who was just 19 years old.

A27. Tottenham managed to score a record 74 goals in the 2017/18 Premier League season.

A28. During the 2010/11 season Spurs became the first team to score two or more goals in every Champions League group game.

A29. Darren Anderton holds the record for most number of Premier League appearances for Tottenham Hotspur appearing 299 times in total, from August 1992 to March 2004.

A30. Harry Kane has scored the most number of hat tricks in the Premier League for Spurs, having scored 8 hat tricks for the club prior to the start of the 2019/20 season.

I hope you're getting most of the answers right. Let's move onto the next set of questions.

31. How many times have Tottenham Hotspur won the Football League First Division?
    A. 2
    B. 3
    C. 4

32. How many times have Tottenham Hotspur won the FA Cup?
    A. 6
    B. 7
    C. 8

33. How many times have Tottenham Hotspur won the League Cup?
    A. 2
    B. 3
    C. 4

34. How many times have Tottenham Hotspur won a European trophy?
    A. 1
    B. 2
    C. 3

35. In which year did Tottenham Hotspur win their first League trophy?
    A. 1930/31
    B. 1950/51
    C. 1960/61

36.   In which year did Tottenham Hotspur win their first FA Cup?
   A. 1901
   B. 1931
   C. 1951

37.   In which year did Tottenham Hotspur win their first League Cup?
   A. 1970
   B. 1971
   C. 1972

38.   In which season did Tottenham Hotspur last win the League?
   A. 1960/61
   B. 1970/71
   C. 1980/81

39.   In which season did Tottenham Hotspur last win the League Cup?
   A. 2006
   B. 2007
   C. 2008

40.   In which year did Tottenham Hotspur last win the FA Cup?
   A. 1971
   B. 1981
   C. 1991

Here are the answers to the last set of questions.

A31. Tottenham Hotspur have won the Football League First Division twice.

A32. Spurs have won the FA Cup eight times.

A33. Tottenham have won the League Cup four times: 1970/71, 1972/73, 1998/99 and 2007/08.

A34. Tottenham have won three European trophies. They have won the European Cup Winners Cup once and the UEFA Cup twice.

A35. Tottenham won their first League title in the 1950/51 season.

A36. Tottenham won their first FA Cup in 1901, defeating Sheffield United 3-1 following a 2-2 draw in the final. This was in the days before extra time and penalties. Jack Jones was the captain who lifted the trophy with Spurs becoming the only non-league side to win the FA Cup. This is a record that will probably never be broken.

A37. Tottenham won their first League Cup in 1971.

A38. Tottenham Hotspur's last League trophy came in the 1960/61 season.

A39. Tottenham last won the League Cup on the 24th February 2008, beating Chelsea 2-1 after extra time, at Wembley.

A40. Tottenham last won the FA Cup on the 18th May 1991, at the end of the 1990/91 season. Spurs defeated Nottingham Forest 2-1 with goals from Paul Stewart and an own goal from Forest defender Des Walker in injury time. The match is remembered for a reckless tackle by Paul Gascoigne which resulted in him being stretchered off. Gary Mabbutt was the captain who lifted the trophy on the day.

I hope you're having fun, and getting most of the answers right.

41.What is the record transfer fee paid by Tottenham Hotspur?
    A. £35 million
    B. £45 million
    C. £55 million

42. For which player did Tottenham Hotspur pay the record transfer fee?
    A. Tanguy Ndombele
    B. Davinson Sanchez
    C. Moussa Sissoko

43. What is the record transfer fee received by Tottenham Hotspur?
    A. £81.3 million
    B. £83.3 million
    C. £85.3 million

44. What is the name of the player for which the record transfer fee was received?
    A. Gareth Bale
    B. Dimitar Berbatov
    C. Luka Modric

45. Where was Victor Wanyama born?
    A. Ghana
    B. Kenya
    C. Nigeria

46. Who is the youngest ever England international whilst a player at the club?
   A. Jimmy Dimmock
   B. Jimmy Greaves
   C. Aaron Lennon

47. Who has scored the fastest ever hat trick for Spurs?
   A. Jermaine Defoe
   B. Robbie Keane
   C. Teddy Sheringham

48. Who scored direct from a free kick from 88 yards in 2007?
   A. Dimitar Berbatov
   B. David Ginola
   C. Paul Robinson

49. Who is the youngest player ever to represent Tottenham Hotspur?
   A. John Bostock
   B. Steven Caulker
   C. Ally Dick

50. Who is the oldest player ever to represent Tottenham Hotspur?
   A. Jimmy Cantrell
   B. Martin Chivers
   C. Brad Friedel

Here are the answers to the last ten questions.

A41. The most amount of money Tottenham have spent on a single player is £55 million, plus up to an additional £9 million in potential add-ons.

A42. French midfielder Tanguy Ndombele arrived from Lyon in July 2019 for a reported £55 million,

A43. The most amount of money Tottenham have received for the sale of a single player is £85.3 million.

A44. Gareth Bale was sold to Real Madrid on 1st September 2013, and is by far the most expensive player Spurs have ever sold to another club.

A45. Wanyama was born in Nairobi in Kenya.

A46. Aaron Lennon is the club's youngest ever England international, making his debut aged just 19 years and 48 days old for England against Jamaica at Old Trafford on 3rd June 2006.

A47. Jermain Defoe scored a hat trick within seven minutes at home to Wigan Athletic on 22nd November 2009. It was the second fastest hat trick in Premier League history at the time.

A48. Goalkeeper Paul Robinson scored direct form a free kick at home to Watford on 17th March 2007. The distance of 88 yards remains the longest scoring free kick in Premier League history.

A49. On 6th November 2008 John Bostock became the youngest ever player to represent Tottenham Hotspur in a competitive game when he came on as a substitute against Dinamo Zagreb in a UEFA Cup game aged just 16 years and 295 days.

A50. Brad Friedel is the oldest ever player to represent Tottenham Hotspur. His last appearance for the club was in a Premier League game at Newcastle on 10th November 2013 and he was 42 years old at the time! The goalkeeper won 82 caps for the United States before his retirement.

I hope you're learning some new facts about the club.

51. Who is the oldest ever goal scorer for Tottenham Hotspur?
    A. William Gallas
    B. Gustavo Poyet
    C. Teddy Sheringham

52. Who is Tottenham Hotspur's longest serving manager of all time?
    A. Bill Nicholson
    B. Peter McWilliam
    C. Harry Redknapp

53. What bird is on the crest of Tottenham Hotspur?
    A. Buzzard
    B. Cockerel
    C. Eagle

54. What is the name of the match day programme of Tottenham Hotspur?
    A. Catch The Match
    B. Match Day Magazine
    C. Spurs News

55. What nationality is Christian Eriksen?
    A. Danish
    B. Norwegian
    C. Swedish

56.   Which of these is a Tottenham Hotspur fanzine?
   A. The Crafty Cockerel
   B. The Fighting Cock
   C. The Rooster

57.   How many players have played for both Tottenham Hotspur and Arsenal?
   A. 15
   B. 16
   C. 17

58.   What is the motto of Tottenham Hotspur?
   A. Dare to do the impossible
   B. To dare is to do
   C. He who dares wins

59.   What is Erik Lamela's nickname?
   A. Chopper
   B. Coco
   C. Crackle

60.   What song did Chas and Dave record about Tottenham Hotspur?
   A. Ossie's Dream
   B. Come On You Spurs
   C. Here at The Lane

Here are the answers to the last set of questions.

A51. Teddy Sheringham holds the record for being the oldest goal scorer for the club. He scored aged 37 years and 19 days in a 3-2 win at West Bromwich Albion on 21st April 2003.

A52. Bill Nicholson remains the longest serving manager of all time for Spurs. He was in change for 832 games in total from 1958 to 1974.

A53. Since the 1921 FA Cup final the Tottenham Hotspur crest has featured a cockerel. Harry Hotspur wore riding spurs and his fighting cocks were fitted with spurs which can be seen in the crests from the early 1920s. Prior to that, in 1909 a bronze cast of cockerel standing on a football was placed on top of the West Stand at the old ground and since then the cockerel and ball have been a major part of the club's identity.

A54. The name of the match day program is The Official Match Day Magazine.

A55. Eriksen was born in Middelfart, Denmark.

A56. The Fighting Cock is perhaps the best known of the Spurs fanzines, and it now produces podcasts on a regular basis for today's digital audience.

A57. There have been 15 players to play for both Spurs and Arsenal. The last player to do so was Emmanuel Adebayor.

A58. The club's Latin motto is "Audere est Facere" which in English means "To Dare Is to Do".

A59. Erik Lamela's nickname is Coco. It means bogeyman in Latin America!

A60. 'Ossie's Dream' was a single recorded by Chas and Dave back in 1981, and it reached number 5 in the charts. The chorus starts with "Spurs are on their way to Wembley". The title refers to former player Osvaldo Ardiles.

Let's give you some easy questions.

61. What is the traditional colour of Tottenham Hotspur's home shirt?
    A. Blue
    B. Red
    C. White

62. What is the traditional colour of Tottenham Hotspur's away shirt?
    A. Black
    B. Green
    C. Yellow

63. Who is Tottenham Hotspur's current shirt sponsor?
    A. AIA
    B. ABA
    C. AON

64. Who were the first official sponsors of Tottenham Hotspur's shirt?
    A. Holsten
    B. HP
    C. Kappa

65. Which of these holiday companies once sponsored the club?
    A. Thomas Cook
    B. Thomson Holidays
    C. Tui

66. What is the name of Tottenham Hotspur's current executive chairman?
   A. Daniel Ashley
   B. Daniel Craig
   C. Daniel Levy

67. Who won the Wembley goal of the century award in 2001?
   A. Nico Claesen
   B. Mauricio Taricco
   C. Ricardo Villa

68. Who was the club's first ever black player?
   A. John Cameron
   B. Walter Tull
   C. Arthur Turner

69. Against which team did Tottenham Hotspur play their first ever competitive game?
   A. Barnet
   B. St. Albans
   C. Royal Arsenal

70. Which player won the supporters' player of the year award for the 2018/19 season?
   A. Heung Min-Son
   B. Christian Eriksen
   C. Jan Vertonghen

Here is the latest set of answers.

A61. The traditional colour of Tottenham's home shirt is of course white.

A62. The traditional colour of Tottenham's away kit is not so easy, so take a point for either black or yellow.

A63. AIA are the current shirt sponsors. They are a provider of insurance services.

A64. Holsten was the first official shirt sponsor of Tottenham Hotspur, back in 1983.

A65. Thomson Holidays sponsored the club from 2002 to 2006.

A66. Daniel Levy is the current chairman of the club.

A67. Ricardo Villa scored an amazing goal for Spurs against Manchester City in the Fa Cup Final replay in 1981 which was later awarded the Wembley goal of the century award. Club legend Ricky Villa joined the club in the summer of 1978 after winning the World Cup with Argentina. He was a remarkable player, and he even scored on his Spurs debut.

A68. Walter Tull was the first ever black player to play for Tottenham Hotspur. He played ten games between 1909 and 1911. Unfortunately, he was killed on active service in the First World War.

A69. Tottenham played their first ever competitive game against St. Albans beating them 5-2 in the 1st round of the London Association Cup, on 17th October 1885.

A70. Heung-Min Son won the player of the year award for the 2018/19 season. Deservedly so.

Here is the next batch of questions to test your knowledge.

71. In which year did Tottenham Hotspur first win the UEFA Cup?
   A. 1970
   B. 1971
   C. 1972

72. In which year did Tottenham Hotspur win the European Cup Winners Cup?
   A. 1963
   B. 1968
   C. 1973

73. What is the club's official twitter account?
   A. @SpursOfficial
   B. @THFC
   C. @Tottenham

74. What shirt number does Dele Alli wear?
   A. 10
   B. 20
   C. 30

75. Who is the captain for the 2019/20 season?
   A. Harry Kane
   B. Hugo Lloris
   C. Jan Vertonghen

76. How many goals did Jürgen Klinsmann score for the club in total?
   A. 29
   B. 39
   C. 49

77. Which manager developed the famous "push and run" tactical style of play?
   A. Osvaldo Ardiles
   B. Glenn Hoddle
   C. Arthur Rowe

78. In what year did Tottenham Hotspur start wearing shirt numbers?
   A. 1938
   B. 1939
   C. 1940

79. Who are Tottenham Hotspur's current kit manufacturers?
   A. Adidas
   B. Nike
   C. Under Armour

80. Which of these has never supplied kit to Tottenham?
   A. Admiral
   B. Hummel
   C. New Balance

Here are the answers to the last set of questions.

A71. Tottenham first won the inaugural UEFA Cup in 1972. The final was a two-legged affair against Wolverhampton Wanderers which Spurs won 3-2 on aggregate.

A72. Tottenham won the European Cup Winners Cup in 1963.

A73. @SpursOfficial is the club's official twitter account. It tweets multiple times daily and it has over three million followers.

A74. Milton Keynes born midfielder Alli wears the number 20 shirt.

A75. Goalkeeper Lloris started the 2019/20 campaign as captain, with Kane as the vice-captain.

A76. The legend that is Jürgen Klinsmann managed to score 30 goals for Spurs in 50 games in the 1994/95 season. In his second spell at the club, he scored 9 goals in 15 games in the 1997/98 season. So in total he scored 39 goals for the club.

A77. "Push and Run" also known as a one-two, a wall-pass or a give-and-go was a tactic developed by Arthur Rowe. It proved an effective way to move the ball at pace, with players' positions begin fluid. Implementing this new style, Spurs ran away with their first ever League title in 1951.

A78. Shirt numbers were first introduced in 1939.

A79. Nike is the current kit manufacturer of Tottenham Hotspur. The deal is rumoured to be worth £25 million a season to the club.

A80. New Balance has never supplied kit to Tottenham, whereas Admiral and Hummel amongst many others have.

Here are the next set of questions, let's hope you get most of them right.

81.   How many times have Tottenham Hotspur won the UEFA Cup?
         A. 1
         B. 2
         C. 3

82.   Who has scored the most European goals for Tottenham Hotspur?
         A. Gareth Bale
         B. Jermaine Defoe
         C. Harry Kane

83.   What is Tottenham Hotspur's highest transfer fee received for an English player?
         A. £33 million
         B. £43 million
         C. £53 million

84.   The fee was received for which player?
         A. Darren Bent
         B. Michael Carrick
         C. Kyle Walker

85.   Who has scored the most goals in the league for Tottenham Hotspur during the Premier League era?
         A. Harry Kane
         B. Robbie Keane
         C. Teddy Sheringham

86.　　Who is the most capped player while at the club?
　　A. Danny Blanchflower
　　B. Pat Jennings
　　C. Gary Lineker

87.　　In which year did Spurs last play in the Second Division?
　　A. 1977/78
　　B. 1978/79
　　C. 1979/80

88.　　Which manager led Tottenham Hotspur to victory in the Cup Winners' Cup in 1963?
　　A. Jimmy Anderson
　　B. Terry Neill
　　C. Bill Nicholson

89.　　What team did they beat in the 1963 European Cup Winners' Cup Final?
　　A. AC Milan
　　B. Atletico Madrid
　　C. Valencia

90.　　What was the score in the 1963 European Cup Winners' Cup final?
　　A. 3-1
　　B. 4-1
　　C. 5-1

Here are the answers to the last set of questions.

A81. Spurs have won the UEFA Cup twice in their history. The second such victory was a two legged final against Anderlecht in 1984 which was decided on penalties after the sides had drawn 2-2 on aggregate. There were many heroes in the team, including captain Graham Roberts, but most credit goes to goalkeeper Tony Parks for saving the final penalty kick, and winning Spurs the trophy. It is worth tracking down footage of the second leg on YouTube to see the sheer drama of it all.

A82. Harry Kane is Tottenham's leading goal scorer in Europe with 24 goals prior to the start of the 2019/20 season.

A83. The highest transfer fee received by Spurs for an English player is £53 million.

A84. £53 million was received from Manchester City for defender Kyle Walker in July 2017. This figure comfortably beat the previous record of £18.6 million for the sale of central midfielder Michael Carrick which had stood since 2006.

A85. Harry Kane is the club's top goal scorer since the start of the Premier League era scoring 128 goals in the Premier League for the club in total as at 1st September 2019. Teddy Sheringham is second on the all-time list with 97 goals.

A86. Pat Jennings won the most caps while at the club, being capped 74 times for Northern Ireland.

A87. Tottenham Hotspur last played in the Second Division during the 1977/78 season.

A88. It was Bill Nicholson who led Spurs to victory in the European Cup Winners' Cup in 1963.

A89. Spurs beat Atletico Madrid in the 1963 European Cup Winners' Cup final.

A90. Spurs stuffed Atletico Madrid 5-1 in the final in Rotterdam. The victory made them the first British team to win a major European trophy.

Here we go then with the last batch of questions.

91. Who was the top goal scorer for the club in the 2018/19 season?
    A. Christian Eriksen
    B. Son Heung-min
    C. Harry Kane

92. What shirt number did Gary Mabbutt normally wear for Spurs?
    A. 4
    B. 5
    C. 6

93. Which club was Jimmy Greaves sold to?
    A. A.C. Milan
    B. Chelsea
    C. West Ham United

94. What is Tottenham's record victory in the Premier League era?
    A. 7-1
    B. 8-1
    C. 9-1

95. Who was the first ever Spurs manager?
    A. Frank Brettell
    B. John Cameron
    C. Fred Kirkham

96. In which year was Jürgen Klinsmann voted as Tottenham's Player of the Year?

A. 1994
B. 1997
C. 1998

97.   Who is considered as Tottenham's greatest keeper of all time?
A. Bill Brown
B. Ray Clemence
C. Pat Jennings

98.   What was John White's nickname?
A. The Ghost
B. The Phantom
C. The Shadow

99.   What is the club's official website address?
A. spurs.com
B. spursfc.com
C. tottenhamhotspur.com

100.   Who is considered as Tottenham Hotspur's greatest captain of all time?
A. Danny Blanchflower
B. Ron Burgess
C. Ledley King

101.   Who can be considered the most successful ever Spurs manager?
A. Glenn Hoddle
B. Bill Nicholson
C. Harry Redknapp

Here are the answers to the final set of questions.

A91. Harry Kane was the leading goal scorer for the 2018/19 season. He scored 17 goals in the Premier League and 7 in the various cup competitions, so 24 goals in total for the season.

A92. The legend that is Gary Mabbutt normally wore number six.

A93. Jimmy Greaves was sold to West Ham United in 1971.

A94. On 22nd November 2009, Spurs thrashed Wigan Athletic 9-1 to record their highest Premier League win. So far.

A95. Frank Brettell was appointed manager in March 1898 - the first ever Spurs manager.

A96. Jürgen Klinsmann was voted as Tottenham's Player of the Year in 1994.

A97. The legend that is Pat Jennings is considered as Tottenham's greatest goalkeeper of all time.

A98. Scottish international John White played a significant role in the 1960/61 Double winning side. He was nicknamed The Ghost because he was elusive and impossible to man mark, and often arrived unexpectedly in the opposition's penalty area. He was tragically killed by a lightning strike in 1964 aged just 27 years old.

A99. tottenhamhotspur.com is the club's official website address.

A100. Danny Blanchflower is considered as Tottenham's greatest captain of all time. He led the side to the Double in 1961 and also the European Cup Winners Cup in 1963. He was twice voted the Football Writers Association Player of the Year.

A101. The incomparable Bill Nicholson is the most successful manager Spurs have ever had. With him as manager, Spurs won the League, the FA Cup three times, the League Cup twice, the UEFA Cup and the European Cup Winners Cup. His record is unlikely to ever be broken.

That's it. That's a great question to finish with. I hope you enjoyed this book, and I hope you got most of the answers right.

I also hope you learnt some new facts about the club, and if you spotted anything wrong, or have a general comment, please visit the glowwormpress.com website and send us a message.

Thanks for reading, and if you did enjoy the book, would you please leave a positive review on Amazon.

Made in the USA
Middletown, DE
21 November 2019

79135638R00028